U.S. ENVIRONMENTAL PROTECTION AGENCY

OFFICE OF INSPECTOR GENERAL

Weaknesses in EPA's Management of the Radiation Network System Demand Attention

Report No. 12-P-0417   April 19, 2012

Scan this mobile
code to learn more
about the EPA OIG.

Report Contributors: Richard Eyermann
                                             Mike Davis
                                             Jim Haller
                                             Marcia Hirt-Reigeluth
                                             Jennifer Hutkoff
                                             Yeon Kim
                                             Heather Layne

Abbreviations

CIPP	Critical Infrastructure and Key Resources Protection Plan
CO	Contracting officer
COR	Contracting officer representative
CPARS	Contractor Performance Assessment Reporting System
CPS	Contractor Performance System
EPA	U.S. Environmental Protection Agency
EPAAR	Environmental Protection Agency Acquisition Regulations
FAR	Federal Acquisition Regulation
GFP	Government-furnished property
MATS	Management Audit Tracking System
MPR	Monthly progress report
NAREL	National Air and Radiation Environmental Laboratory
NIH	National Institutes of Health
OAM	Office of Acquisition Management
OAR	Office of Air and Radiation
OIG	Office of Inspector General
ORIA	Office of Radiation and Indoor Air
PPIRS	Past Performance Information Retrieval System
QAPP	Quality Assurance Project Plan
RadNet	Radiation Network
SOW	Statement of work

Cover photo: Stationary RadNet monitor. (EPA photo)

At a Glance

Why We Did This Review

The U.S. Environmental Protection Agency (EPA) Office of Inspector General (OIG) sought to determine whether EPA is following quality control procedures to ensure that data submitted from Radiation Network (RadNet) monitors nationwide are reliable and accurate, and whether EPA effectively implemented corrective actions in response to the EPA OIG's January 27, 2009, audit report on RadNet.

Background

EPA's December 2004 Critical Infrastructure and Key Resources Protection Plan identified RadNet monitors as critical infrastructure. The mission of RadNet is to monitor environmental radioactivity in the United States to provide high-quality data for assessing public exposure and environmental impacts resulting from nuclear emergencies, and to provide baseline data during routine conditions. RadNet played a critical role in monitoring radiation levels in the United States during the March 2011 Japan nuclear incident.

For further information, contact our Office of Congressional and Public Affairs at (202) 566-2391.

The full report is at:
www.epa.gov/oig/reports/2012/
20120419-12-P-0417.pdf

Weaknesses in EPA's Management of the Radiation Network System Demand Attention

What We Found

Broken RadNet monitors and late filter changes impaired this critical infrastructure asset. On March 11, 2011, at the time of the Japan nuclear incident, 25 of the 124 installed RadNet monitors, or 20 percent, were out of service for an average of 130 days. The service contractor completed repairs for all monitors by April 8, 2011. In addition, 6 of the 12 RadNet monitors we sampled had gone over 8 weeks without a filter change, and 2 of those for over 300 days. Because EPA managed RadNet with lower than required priority, parts shortages and insufficient contract oversight contributed to extensive delays in fixing broken monitors. In addition, broken RadNet monitors and relaxed quality controls contributed to the filters not being changed timely. Out-of-service monitors and unchanged filters may reduce the quality and availability of critical data needed to assess radioactive threats to public health and the environment.

EPA remains behind schedule for installing the RadNet monitors and did not fully resolve contracting issues identified in the OIG's January 2009 report. Until EPA improves contractor oversight, the Agency's ability to use RadNet data to protect human health and the environment, and meet requirements established in the National Response Framework for Nuclear Radiological Incidents, is potentially impaired.

What We Recommend

We recommend that the Assistant Administrator for Air and Radiation establish and enforce expectations for RadNet operations readiness. We recommend improved planning and management of parts availability, monitoring of filter replacement and operators, and monitoring of the installation of the remaining RadNet monitors. Further, we recommend that the Assistant Administrator, in conjunction with the Assistant Administrator for Administration and Resources Management, hold contractors accountable by establishing milestones, using incentives and disincentives, requiring contracting officers and contracting officers' representatives to formally evaluate RadNet contractors annually, and ensure that the Agency's Management Audit Tracking System is accurate and current. The Agency concurred with the recommendations except for developing metrics for evaluating frequency of filter changes and completing contractor performance evaluations, which is considered unresolved. The Agency also proposed revised language, which we incorporated where appropriate.

UNITED STATES ENVIRONMENTAL PROTECTION AGENCY
WASHINGTON, D.C. 20460

April 19, 2012

MEMORANDUM

SUBJECT: Weaknesses in EPA's Management of the
Radiation Network System Demand Attention
Report No. 12-P-0417

FROM: Arthur A. Elkins, Jr.

TO: Gina McCarthy
Assistant Administrator for Air and Radiation

Craig E. Hooks
Assistant Administrator for Administration and Resources Management

This is our report on the subject audit conducted by the Office of Inspector General (OIG) of the U.S. Environmental Protection Agency (EPA). This report contains findings that describe the problems the OIG has identified and corrective actions the OIG recommends. This report represents the opinion of the OIG and does not necessarily represent the final EPA position. Final determinations on matters in this report will be made by EPA managers in accordance with established audit resolution procedures.

Action Required

In accordance with EPA Manual 2750, you are required to provide a written response to this report within 90 calendar days. Your response will be posted on the OIG's public website, along with our comments on your response. Your response should be provided in an Adobe PDF file that complies with the accessibility requirements of Section 508 of the Rehabilitation Act of 1973, as amended. If your response contains data that you do not want to be released to the public, you should identify the data for redaction. You should include a corrective actions plan for agreed-upon actions, including milestone dates. We have no objections to the further release of this report to the public. This report will be available at http://www.epa.gov/oig.

If you or your staff have any questions regarding this report, please contact Melissa Heist, Assistant Inspector General for Audit, at (202) 566- 0899 heist.melissa@epa.gov; or Mike Davis, Acting Director for Efficiency Audits, at (513) 487-2363 or davis.michaeld@epa.gov.

Table of Contents

Chapters

Appendices

-continued-

Chapter 1
Introduction

Purpose

In January 2009, the Office of Inspector General (OIG) issued an audit report that contained recommendations for improving the management and oversight of the U.S. Environmental Protection Agency's (EPA's) Radiation Network (RadNet) system. The nature and importance of the prior report recommendations and the recent attention on RadNet due to the critical role it played in the United States during the March 2011 Japan nuclear incident warranted a follow-up audit. Our audit objectives were to determine:

- Whether EPA is following quality control procedures to ensure that data submitted from the RadNet monitors nationwide are reliable and accurate

- Whether EPA effectively implemented corrective actions in response to our January 27, 2009, audit report, *EPA Plans for Managing Counter Terrorism/Emergency Response Equipment and Protecting Critical Assets Not Fully Implemented*

Background

The Patriot Act of 2001 defined critical infrastructure as assets so vital to the United States that their incapacity or destruction would have a debilitating impact on public health or safety. Homeland Security Presidential Directive No. 7, December 17, 2003, required federal agencies to identify, prioritize, and protect Critical Infrastructure and Key Resources Protection Plan (CIPP) assets. EPA's December 2004 CIPP identified RadNet monitors as critical infrastructure. The June 2008 Nuclear/Radiological Incident Annex to the National Response Framework lists EPA and RadNet as a key federal radiological resource and asset.

EPA's RadNet System

RadNet, a national network of monitoring stations, provides real-time monitoring of environmental levels of radiation in the United States. Monitoring stations regularly collect air, precipitation, drinking water, and milk samples for analysis of radioactivity. RadNet has three objectives:

Stationary RadNet monitor. (EPA OIG photo)

- Provide data for nuclear emergency response assessments
- Provide data on ambient levels of radiation in the environment for baseline and trend analysis
- Inform the general public and public officials about radiation levels

EPA's RadNet system consists of 124 stationary (fixed) monitors[1] and 40 deployable air monitors that can be sent to take readings anywhere in the country (figure 1). Our audit focused on EPA's stationary RadNet air monitoring system.

Figure 1: Locations of RadNet monitors nationwide as of April 2011

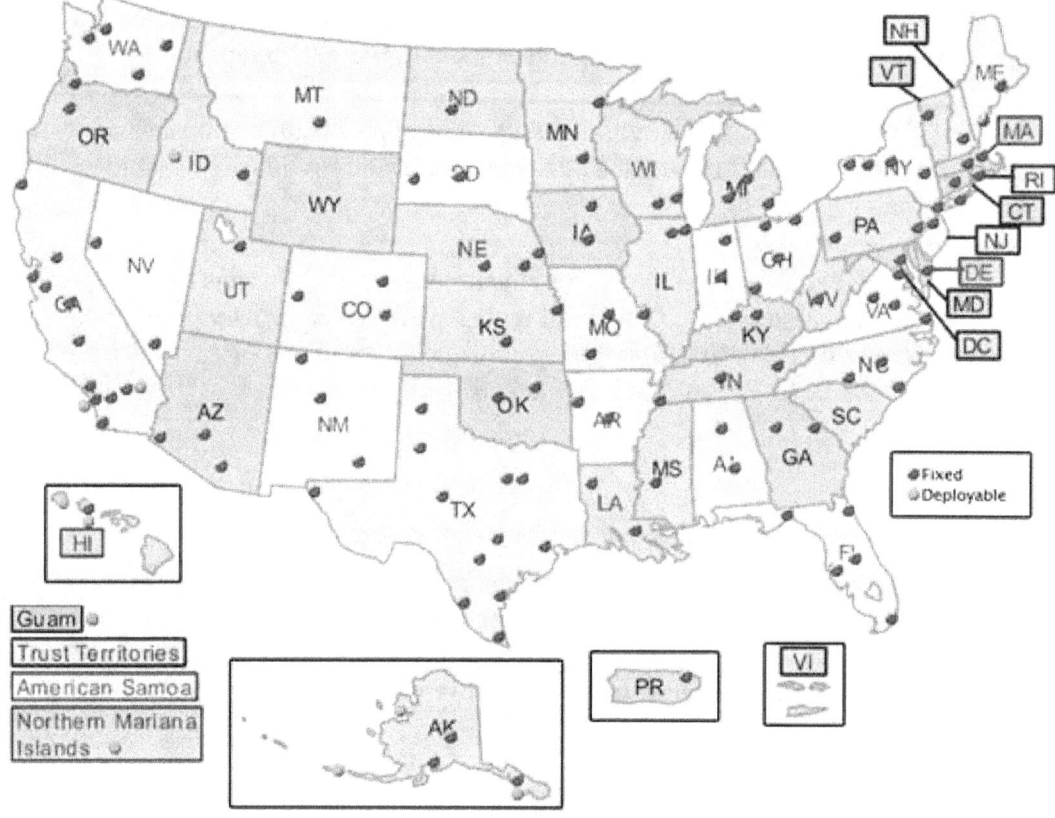

Source: EPA Japan Nuclear Emergency: Radiation Monitoring website, http://www.epa.gov/japan2011/rert/radnet-data-map.html/.

---

[1] Stationary monitors collect information on air particulates. When fully implemented, the RadNet system will consist of 134 stationary monitors. The remaining 10 monitors are planned to be installed, by June 2012, in Boise City, Idaho; Casper, Wyoming; Champaign, Illinois; Charleston, South Carolina; Great Falls, Montana; Greensboro, North Carolina; LaCrosse, Wisconsin; Scranton, Pennsylvania; Shawano, Wisconsin; and St. George, Utah.

RadNet monitors measure airborne radiation collected on filters 24 hours a day, 7 days a week, and submit data for analysis to the EPA National Air and Radiation Environmental Laboratory (NAREL) in Montgomery, Alabama. NAREL is part of the Office of Air and Radiation (OAR), Office of Radiation and Indoor Air (ORIA). These data allow NAREL to identify normal background radiation levels in an area. A computer continually reviews the real-time air monitoring data and, if the results show an increase in radiation levels outside of the normal range, the computer immediately alerts EPA laboratory staff so they can review the data to ensure accuracy. Operators of the fixed monitors also send filters to NAREL for further analysis. The detailed filter analysis allows NAREL to see the trace amounts of radioactive material that the real-time air monitors do not pick up.

NAREL worked with the EPA Office of Acquisition Management (OAM) to award the three contracts that are the subject of this review—one each for the manufacture of stationary air monitors,[2] repair and maintenance services, and ordering of needed spare and repair parts. These contracts are crucial to the success of the RadNet program. OAM awarded the three contracts from 2007 to 2010, and they have a total contract obligation value of over $8 million (table 1). The contracts for fixed air monitoring stations and spare parts were awarded to the same contractor due to the proprietary nature of those spare parts.

Table 1: RadNet contracts covered by this review

RadNet contract no.	Purpose of contract	Award date	Total contract obligations
EP-W-07-076	Fixed air monitoring stations	09/28/2007	$5,326,210
EP-D-08-068	Repair and maintenance services	05/05/2008	1,489,880
EP-D-10-085	Spare parts	09/21/2010	1,405,913
		Total	$8,222,003

Source: EPA Active Contract Listing and Financial Data Warehouse as of February 9, 2012.

Japan Nuclear Incident

On March 11, 2011, the magnitude 9.0 Tohoku earthquake in northern Japan created a tsunami that damaged the Fukushima nuclear power plant. In response to the Japan nuclear incident, EPA increased sampling frequency and analysis to detect and measure radiation levels, and inform the public of any changes in those levels. EPA also increased sampling frequency for the milk and drinking water networks, and increased analysis frequency for all networks to detect and measure radiation levels. On April 2, 2011, an EPA press release stated that several EPA air monitors detected very low levels of radioactive material in the United States consistent with estimates from the damaged nuclear reactors. EPA explained that these detections were expected, and the levels detected were far below levels of public health concern.

---

[2] OAM awarded earlier RadNet contracts; those contracts are not part of this review.

To provide additional geographic coverage to areas in close proximity to the releases in Japan, EPA shipped deployable monitors to islands in the Pacific, including Guam and the Commonwealth of the Northern Mariana Islands, and to locations in the western United States, including Hawaii, Idaho, and Alaska.

On April 12, 2011, the U.S. Senate Committee on Environment and Public Works held a hearing, "Review of the Nuclear Emergency in Japan and Implications for the U.S.," and the EPA Administrator testified on the systems EPA has in place to protect the American public and environment.

> *Since the events in Japan occurred, EPA's website has had thousands of views and we have received many positive comments from the public on the information we have made available. The Agency will continue to provide [RadNet] monitoring results to the public in a very open and transparent manner. While we do not expect radiation from the damaged Japanese reactors to reach the United States at harmful levels, I want to assure you that EPA will continue our coordination with our federal partners to monitor the air, milk, precipitation and drinking water for any changes, and we will continue our outreach to the public and the elected officials to provide information on our monitoring results.*
>
> Lisa Jackson, EPA Administrator, Testimony Before the United States Senate, Committee on Environment and Public Works, April 12, 2011.

On May 3, 2011, EPA announced that after a thorough data review showing declining radiation levels related to the Japan nuclear incident, it had returned to the routine RadNet sampling and analysis processes.

Prior EPA OIG Reports

On April 26, 2006, the OIG issued Report No. 2006-P-00022, *EPA Needs to Better Implement Plan for Protecting Critical Infrastructure and Key Resources Used to Respond to Terrorist Attacks and Disasters.* We reported that EPA listed RadNet in the CIPP and prioritized it as the fourth-most-important item. We identified that the Agency had not completed five CIPP initiatives, including RadNet. We recommended that the Deputy Administrator establish program office accountability for implementing each CIPP initiative as well as milestones, with short- and long-term performance measures for monitoring the implementation of each CIPP initiative. The Agency agreed with the recommendations and established accountability with the Office of Solid Waste and Emergency Response for coordinating all activities related to the CIPP. EPA planned to begin the first phase of deployment for the fixed RadNet monitors in 2006, with completion scheduled in fiscal year 2009.

On January 27, 2009, the OIG issued Report No. 09-P-0087, *EPA Plans for Managing Counter Terrorism/Emergency Response Equipment and Protecting Critical Assets Not Fully Implemented*. We reported that EPA was behind schedule in implementing RadNet, encountered delays and problems with the administration of the contract for the monitors, and may need to modify installed monitors after completing tests of the design. We recommended that EPA monitor the RadNet contract, develop a schedule for addressing design concerns with the monitor, and oversee the implementation of RadNet against the planned schedule until completed. EPA agreed with the recommendations.

An analysis of prior EPA OIG report recommendations is in appendix A.

Noteworthy Achievements

EPA has made progress in implementing the RadNet CIPP initiative since the OIG's 2006 and 2009 audit reports. As of May 2011, EPA had installed 124 of the 134 monitors it ordered, and it completed a test of the RadNet design. The test determined that a change to the installed monitors was not required.

Scope and Methodology

We conducted this performance audit in accordance with generally accepted government auditing standards. Those standards require that we plan and perform the audit to obtain sufficient, appropriate evidence to provide a reasonable basis for our findings and conclusions based on our review objectives. We believe that the evidence obtained provides a reasonable basis for our findings and conclusions based on our audit objectives.

We conducted the audit from May to December 2011. We visited OAM's Headquarters Procurement Operations Division in Washington, DC; OAM's Procurement Operations Division in Research Triangle Park, North Carolina; and NAREL in Montgomery, Alabama.

We interviewed the directors for ORIA and NAREL. We interviewed contracting officers (COs) and the RadNet operations manager to follow up on prior report recommendations and agreed-to corrective actions. We conducted interviews with operators for 12 RadNet monitors to determine whether they followed quality control procedures to ensure that data submitted from the monitors were reliable. We selected a random sample of 12 monitors from the 124 installed to identify a population of monitors to analyze for frequency of filter changes and to identify which operators to interview.

We reviewed prior audit reports, the EPA 2011–2015 Strategic Plan, OAR's 2011–2012 National Program Manager Guidance, and pertinent laws and regulations. We reviewed information in the Agency's Management Audit Tracking System (MATS), and the CO and contracting officer representative

(COR) files, to determine whether EPA implemented corrective actions to address the recommendations pertaining to RadNet in our 2009 audit report. We reviewed the 2010 and 2012 RadNet Quality Assurance Project Plans (QAPPs) to determine the quality control procedures EPA had to ensure that data submitted from the RadNet are reliable. We reviewed the fiscal years 2010 and 2011 Federal Managers' Financial Integrity Act Annual Assurance Letters for EPA's Office of Homeland Security (within the Office of the Administrator) and OAR to determine whether those two letters identified any weaknesses related to the RadNet program. The letters did not identify such weaknesses.

Chapter 2
EPA Not Managing RadNet as a
High-Priority Program

Broken RadNet monitors and late filter changes impaired this critical infrastructure asset. On March 11, 2011, at the time of the Japan nuclear incident, 25 of the 124 installed RadNet monitors, or 20 percent, were out of service for an average of 130 days. In addition, 6 of the 12 RadNet monitors we sampled (50 percent) had gone over 8 weeks without a filter change, and 2 had gone unchanged for over 300 days because they were broken. Unless EPA grants an extension, the repair services contract requires a service contractor to fix broken monitors within 14 days of EPA's notification that a monitor is out of service. The EPA 2010 QAPP required operators to change filters on fixed RadNet real-time monitors twice a week. Because EPA did not manage RadNet as a high-priority program, parts shortages and insufficient contract oversight contributed to the extensive delay in fixing broken monitors. Out-of-service monitors and unchanged filters may reduce the availability and quality of critical data needed to assess radioactive threats to public health and the environment.

Contract and QAAP Define Repair and Filter Change Time Frames

EPA included terms and conditions in the RadNet repair and maintenance services contract to define the period of time for repair. In May 2008, EPA awarded a RadNet repair and maintenance service contract that requires the contractor to fix broken monitors within 14 days of being notified by the COR. EPA may permit an extension of this 14-day period for a specific repair for reasons including unavailability of government-furnished property (GFP), operator unavailability, and physical disruption of the site. EPA acquires the GFP from the contractor that was awarded the propriety spare parts contract.

EPA's 2010 QAPP states that RadNet air station operators collect air particulate filters twice a week and mail the filters via the U.S. Postal Service to NAREL for analysis. When elevated levels of radioactivity are anticipated or known to exist, EPA may request RadNet station operators to increase the sampling frequency and use priority shipping.

One in Five RadNet Monitors Out of Service an Average of 130 Days

At the time of the Japan nuclear incident, 25 of the 124 installed monitors, or 20 percent, were out of service for an average of 130 days (appendix B and figure 2). The 25 out-of-service monitors were located throughout the country, except for the northwest portions of the United States (figure 3).

Figure 2: Length of time RadNet monitors had been broken at time of the Japan nuclear incident

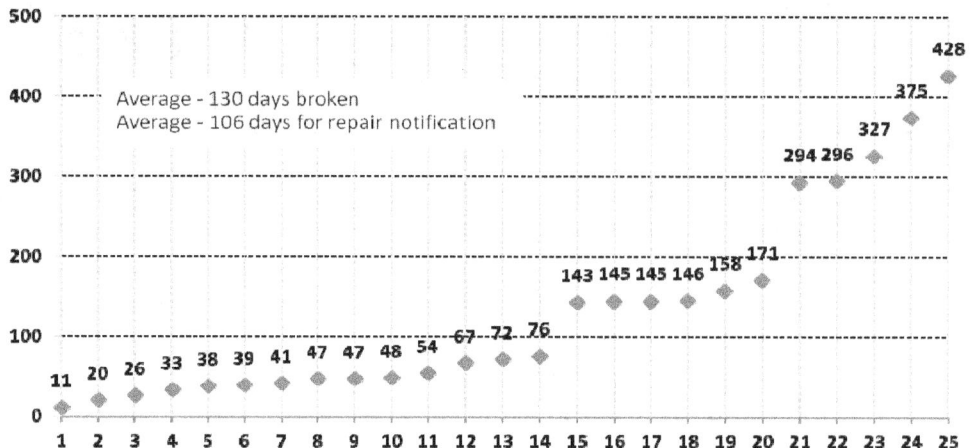

Average - 130 days broken
Average - 106 days for repair notification

Source: OIG analysis of 25 out-of-service monitors per information provided by EPA.

Figure 3: Map of 25 monitors out of service at the time of the Japan nuclear incident

Source: OIG-developed map using Geographic Information System and Agency-provided information on broken monitors.

While the RadNet repair services contract requires the contractor to make the repair within 14 days of being notified by EPA, unless extended, EPA permitted 9 of the 25 monitors to remain out of service for more than 140 days because it did not notify the contractor until parts were available. In addition, two monitors were out of service because no operator was available (table 2).

Table 2: Monitors broken and out of service for more than 140 days

Monitor location	Date out of service	Date back in service	Days out of service
Harlingen, TX	01/28/10	04/01/11	428
Raleigh, NC	03/29/10	04/08/11	375
Fort Wayne, IN	05/02/10	03/25/11	327
Carlsbad, NM*	06/01/10	03/24/11	296
St. Louis, MO	06/09/10	03/30/11	294
Corpus Christi, TX*	10/01/10	03/21/11	171
Oklahoma City, OK	10/17/10	03/24/11	158
Burlington, VT	11/02/10	03/28/11	146
Fort Smith, AR	11/06/10	03/31/11	145
San Diego, CA	10/26/10	03/20/11	145
St. Paul, MN	11/08/10	03/31/11	143

*No operator available.
Source: OIG analysis of 25 out-of-service monitors per information provided by EPA.

EPA took an average of 106 days to notify the service contractor about the out-of-service monitors. EPA justified the delayed repairs and late notification as being due to the unavailability of GFP. EPA did not have the required parts to provide to the repair contractor, and would not for an extended period of time. Therefore, EPA did not notify the contractor that these monitors were in need of repair.

EPA was not able to furnish the parts required for repair of 22 monitors in a timely manner, had not been able to recruit replacement volunteer operators for 2 monitors, and was able to troubleshoot the problem with the remaining monitor without needing to supply replacement parts.

For 8 of the 25 monitors, the EPA COR took 120 to 421 days to notify the repair contractor (table 3).

Table 3: Number of days for EPA to notify contractor of needed repairs

Monitor location	Date out of service	Notification date	Days to notification
Harlingen, TX	01/28/10	03/25/11	421
Raleigh, NC	03/29/10	03/26/11	362
Fort Wayne, IN	05/02/10	03/20/11	322
St. Louis, MO	06/09/10	03/19/11	283
Oklahoma City, OK	10/17/10	03/19/11	153
Burlington, VT	11/02/10	03/20/11	138
Fort Smith, AR	11/06/10	03/24/11	138
San Diego, CA	10/26/10	02/23/11	120

Source: OIG analysis of eight out-of-service monitors per EPA information.

The 25 out-of-service monitors received EPA's priority attention only after the Japan nuclear emergency. The priority attention consisted of cannibalizing monitors under construction for their parts, which were used to repair broken monitors. By April 8, 2011, the service contractor had completed repairs on all monitors (figure 4).

Figure 4: Timeline to fix the 25 monitors after the Japan nuclear incident

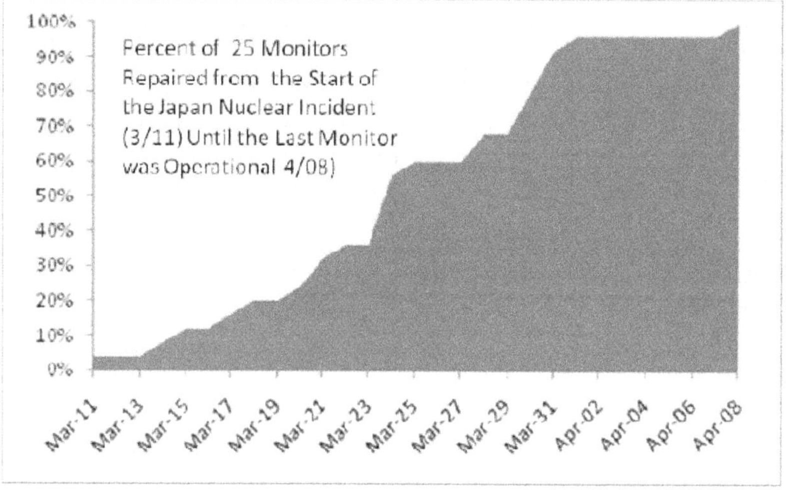

Source: OIG analysis of 25 out-of-service monitors per information provided by EPA.

Filters for RadNet Monitors Not Changed Timely

Operators are not changing filters for the RadNet monitors two times per week as required by the 2010 QAPP. We sampled 12 out of the 124 installed monitors for which we reviewed the frequency of filter changes for the 12-month period May 1, 2010–April 30, 2011 (table 4).

Table 4: Filter changes on random sampling of 12 monitors, May 1, 2010–April 30, 2011

Monitor location	No. of filter changes made	No. of filter changes not made	% not made	Longest elapsed time without filter change in days
Salt Lake City, UT	61	43	41.35%	129
Riverside, CA	98	6	5.77	N/A
Montgomery, AL	103	1	1	N/A
Burlington, VT	3	101	97.12	339
Eureka, CA	55	49	47.12	N/A
Tulsa, OK	38	66	63.46	152
St. Louis, MO	6	98	94.23	309
Richmond, VA	90	14	13.46	21
Fort Worth, TX	65	39	37.50	21
Omaha, NE	38	66	63.46	147
Houston, TX	74	30	28.85	79
Toledo, OH	97	7	6.73	N/A
Average filter changes not made			41.60%	

Source: OIG analysis of 12 random samples; filter change data provided by EPA.

Our review disclosed that:

- Seven of 12 monitors were broken for an extended period and thus did not have filter changes or submit data for 21 to 339 days.
- For the 1-year time span, 42 percent of required filter changes did not occur because of broken monitors or volunteer issues.
- Monitors located in Burlington, Vermont, and St. Louis, Missouri, had only three and six filter changes for the 1-year period, respectively.

Not all operators changed filters twice a week. One operator did not change filters for 309 days because the monitor was broken and unrepaired. Further, because operators are unpaid volunteers from a variety of federal/state/local agencies, universities, and colleges, RadNet filter changes may not be the top priority for all operators. Another operator did not change filters for 339 days because the monitor was broken at one time and the operator had National Guard duty at other times. EPA acknowledged these situations but did not take prompt action. Further, NAREL gave operators permission to wait up to 8 days between filter changes, despite the 2010 QAPP requirement to change the filters twice a week. Some operators requested and NAREL gave permission to change filters once a week. Failure to follow RadNet quality assurance requirements may adversely affect data completeness and potentially impairs RadNet's ability to protect human health.

The 2010 QAPP discussed the twice-per-week filter changes in three separates areas (table 5) and addressed specific elements of the planning and implementation of the real-time radiation monitors, including handling of filter samples collected at the air monitoring sites. EPA's 2001 Requirements for Quality Assurance Project Plans, EPA QA/R-5, explained that QAPPs are important because they establish essential components of assuring the credibility and reliability of Agency data and information. The importance of the QAPP is also defined in the May 2000, *EPA Quality Manual for Environmental Programs* and states:

> The QAPP is a critical planning document for any environmental data operation since it documents how environmental data operations are planned, implemented, documented, and assessed during the life cycle of a program, project, or task. The ultimate success of an environmental program or project depends on the adequacy and sufficiency of the quality of the environmental data collected and used in decision-making. This may depend significantly on the adequacy of the QAPP and its effective implementation.

The *EPA Quality Manual for Environmental Programs* also explains that the QAPP describes the experimental design or data collection design for the project, including as appropriate the types and numbers of samples required, the design of the sampling network, sampling locations and frequencies, sample matrices, measurement parameters of interest, and the rationale for the design.

In response to the draft report, the Agency stated that the frequency of filter changes was not a relevant metric for operational readiness, and stated that the twice weekly filter change referenced in the 2010 QAPP was not intended to be an operational requirement, but rather to provide consistency in throughput at NAREL's analytical laboratory. In March 2012 the Agency revised the QAPP and removed all but one reference to the twice-per-week filter changes. (table 5)

Table 5: Information from the 2010 and 2012 QAPPs on filter changes

Section	QAPP August 6, 2010	QAPP March 8, 2012
8.5.2.2.1	Under routine circumstances, operators send filters, along with field estimates, to NAREL twice weekly from each monitor.	Filters are directly counted for gross beta activity at NAREL.
13.1.13, Step 13	Site operator conducts routine twice-weekly filter changes, field analyses, and filter shipment to NAREL	Site operator conducts routine filter changes and filter shipment to NAREL.
1.3.1.1.2	Current OMB [Office of Management and Budget] reports for the ERAMS [Environmental Radiation Ambient Monitoring System]/RadNet air monitoring network estimate operator expenditure of time to be 75 person-hours per year. This estimate is based on station operators collecting air filters twice per week.	Current OMB reports for the ERAMS/RadNet air monitoring network estimate operator expenditure of time to be 75 person-hours per year. This estimate is based on station operators collecting air filters twice per week. However, less frequent filter changing is common for a variety of logistical reasons and does not affect quality of the data collected by the near-real-time gamma monitoring systems.

Source: EPA's 2010 and 2012 QAPPs.

Since the 2012 QAPP does not specifically define how often filters should be changed, the Agency needs to define at a minimum how often filter changes are needed to provide consistency in throughput at NAREL's analytical laboratory and also develop a matrix for this.

Limited Resources and Competing Priorities Impacted RadNet Readiness

Delayed contract awards and staffing issues negatively affected the full implementation of RadNet. The spare parts contract was awarded long after the warranty expired on the first installed monitor, and the RadNet program is run by a single operations manager who has no backup.

EPA did not prioritize the award of contracts crucial to support the RadNet program. The first RadNet monitor, installed on April 20, 2006, had a 1-year manufacturer's warranty. However, NAREL did not start the process for the parts contract until May 14, 2008, as part of its fiscal year 2010 Acquisition Forecast Plan, which was about 1 year after the manufacturer's warranty expired on the first installed monitor. NAREL submitted the Procurement Initiation Notice on

July 8, 2009, to the Research Triangle Park Procurement Operations Division. Fourteen months after the notice, on September 21, 2010, EPA awarded the parts contract—over 3 years past the warranty expiration date of the first stationary monitor.

The RadNet system is managed by the RadNet Real-Time Air Monitoring operations manager, NAREL. The RadNet operations manager had a variety of responsibilities that competed for prioritization, including but not limited to:

- Network and site management for 124 monitors
- COR for seven RadNet contracts plus another that is pending (including the three contracts that are the subject of this review)
- Quality assurance of RadNet fixed monitor operations

Because of this workload, the operations manager had to make judgments about which issues required action on any particular day. Consequently, the operations manager often deferred activities related to monitor operations, especially those with longer-term impact, instead of treating those activities as a priority. For example, the RadNet operations manager explained that he delayed the following long-term tasks because of the immediate demands he had to address:

- Maintaining operational status of monitors
- Preparing standard operating procedures and quality control documents
- Identifying and preparing sites for installation of monitors
- Implementing and conducting quality assurance activities

The RadNet operations manager has no backup person. The NAREL acting director acknowledged that staffing was a critical area to be resolved, but did not present any specific plans for resolution.

Conclusion

EPA's RadNet program will remain vulnerable until it is managed with the urgency and priority that the Agency reports it to have to its mission, and that is also reflected in the National Response Framework for Nuclear Radiological Incidents. If RadNet is not managed as a high-priority program, EPA may not have the needed data before, during, and after a critical event such as the Japan nuclear incident. Such data are crucial to determine levels of airborne radioactivity that may negatively affect public health and the environment.

Recommendations

We recommend that the Assistant Administrator for Air and Radiation:

1. Establish and enforce written expectations for RadNet operational readiness commensurate with its role in and importance to EPA's mission. Include, at a minimum:

   a. Percentage of stationary monitors expected to be operational.
   b. Maximum length of time stationary monitors are permitted to be nonoperational.
   c. Plan for temporarily backing up broken stationary monitors when operational status is lower than required.
   d. Availability of monitor operators.

2. Implement metrics for RadNet operational readiness to be reviewed daily by NAREL, and periodically by OAR (at least monthly) and by the Deputy Administrator (as needed), to include, at a minimum:

   a. Percentage of monitors operational.
   b. Length of time in nonoperational status.
   c. Need for backup monitors when operational status is too low.
   d. Operator availability.

3. Direct that NAREL improve planning and management for RadNet to include, at a minimum:

   a. Provide for in-stock spare parts to assure operational status established under recommendation 1.
   b. Implement measures to assure that operators are available.
   c. How often filter changes are needed to provide consistency in throughput at NAREL's analytical laboratory and implement a metric for these filter changes.

Agency Response and OIG Evaluation

The Agency concurred with the findings and all but one recommendation, and provided milestone dates for most of the recommendations. The Agency also proposed some revised language, which we incorporated where appropriate in the report. The Agency's full response is in appendix D.

The Agency concurred with recommendations 1.a. through 1.d., and stated that corrective action is expected to be completed by April 1, 2012. We agree with the Agency's corrective actions planned for recommendations 1.a. through 1.d.

The Agency concurred with recommendation 2.a. through 2.d. and stated that corrective action is expected to be completed by April 1, 2012. We agree with the corrective actions planned for recommendation 2.a through 2.d.

The Agency did not agree with our draft report recommendation 2.e. and the need for a performance metric to monitor the frequency of filter changes. The Agency stated the twice weekly filter change referenced in the 2010 QAPP was not intended to be an operational requirement, but rather to provide consistency in throughput at NAREL's analytical laboratory. In March 2012 the Agency revised the QAPP and removed all but one reference to the twice-per-week filter changes. Considering the changes in the 2012 QAPP, we modified and moved recommendation 2.e., to recommendation 3.c., which directs that NAREL improve planning and management for RadNet to include, at a minimum how often filter changes are needed to provide consistency in throughput at NAREL's analytical laboratory and implement a metric for these filter changes, because we believe the Agency needs to define at a minimum, how often filter changes are needed to provide consistency in throughput at NAREL's analytical laboratory.

The Agency concurred with recommendation 3.a. and stated that corrective action was completed. We agree with the Agency's corrective action plan for recommendation 3.a. and request that the Agency include the date corrective actions were completed, the inventory of available spare parts, the budget and future funding for spare parts, and the newly awarded repair contract and the statement of work, as soon as this information is available. Also, the Agency concurred with recommendation 3.b. and stated that corrective action is expected to be completed by April 1, 2012. We agree with the Agency's corrective action for 3b.

Chapter 3
EPA Should Improve
RadNet Contract Oversight

EPA did not fully resolve contracting issues identified in the OIG's January 2009 report. We found that incentives and disincentives for contractors were not included in each of the three RadNet contracts covered by this review, monthly progress reports (MPRs) were not included in terms and conditions of all three contracts, and required contractor performance evaluations were not completed or were late. The OIG's January 2009 report addressed the need to improve contract administration and accountability for the RadNet initiative. EPA concurred with the prior report recommendations and established corrective action plans to monitor and improve contractor performance and oversight issues. The report contained five recommendations, of which EPA has listed four in MATS as completed as of August 2011. However, OIG analysis demonstrated that EPA only completed one of the recommendations (appendix A). As a result, contractor performance issues remained because EPA did not implement prior report recommendations to hold contractors accountable. Until EPA corrects the shortfall in contract oversight, the ability of the RadNet to protect human health and the environment is potentially impaired.

Federal and EPA Guidance Define Contract Management Requirements

Federal and EPA regulation and guidance are available to assist EPA in managing contracts and holding contractors accountable:

- **Federal Acquisition Regulation (FAR) 16.401—Incentive Contracts:** FAR 16.401 discusses the need to provide motivation (incentives) for a contractor to do well. It states that incentive contracts are designed to obtain specific acquisition objectives by including appropriate incentive arrangements designed to (1) motivate contractor efforts that might not otherwise be emphasized, and (2) discourage contractor inefficiency and waste.

- **FAR 16.403—Incentive Contracts:** FAR 16.403 states a fixed-price incentive contract is appropriate when the nature of the supplies or services being acquired and other circumstances of the acquisition are such that the contractor's assumption of a degree of cost responsibility will provide a positive profit incentive for effective cost control and performance.

- **FAR 42.11—Surveillance Requirements:** FAR 42.1104 states that the extent of production surveillance is determined by the contract administration office on the basis of degree of importance to the government, contract requirements for reporting production progress and performance, the contract performance schedule, the contractor's history of contract performance, and the contractor's experience with the contract supplies or services.

- **FAR 42.15—Contractor Performance Information:** FAR 42.1502(c) states that, for each contract and task/delivery order in excess of the simplified acquisition threshold of $150,000, the CO shall annually prepare an evaluation of the contractor's performance.

- **Environmental Protection Agency Acquisition Regulations (EPAAR) Deviation 1542.15 —Contractor Performance Information:**[3] Evaluation reports shall be submitted to the Defense Department's Past Performance Information Retrieval System (PPIRS) through the Web-based Contractor Performance Assessment Reporting System (CPARS), which has connectivity with PPIRS. CPARS replaced the previous reporting system, the National Institutes of Health (NIH) Contractor Performance System (CPS), on May 15, 2010. An evaluation covers each 12-month period after the effective date of the contract or order. EPA's Interim Policy Notice 10-03 required completion of evaluations within 90 business days from the date the CO initiates the evaluation.

Incentives/Disincentives Not Included in All RadNet Contracts

The fixed air monitoring stations contract was the only one of the three in our review that contained an incentive. It was also the only one that included a disincentive; however, we consider that disincentive to be ineffective (table 6).

Table 6: Incentives and disincentives in the three RadNet contracts under review

Contract	Incentive	Disincentive
Fixed air monitoring stations	Yes	Yes, ineffective
Repair service[4]	No	No
Spare parts	No	No

Source: OIG analysis.

---

[3] EPAAR 1542.15, Contractor Performance Information, superseded and rescinded OAM Interim Policy Notice 10-03, effective October 3, 2011.

[4] In the Agency response to the draft report, the Agency stated that 3 days prior to release of our draft report to OAR and OAM, EP-D-I2-003 was awarded on December 12, 2011, for RadNet Air Monitor Maintenance. This contract replaced EP-D-08-068 and does include disincentives for subpar performance as follows: a 5 percent reduction on the invoiced labor amount for every 1 percent slippage from the 95 percent performance level.

The OIG's January 2009 report recommended that the Agency maintain current incentives in the new RadNet contracts and seek opportunities to expand these, and include disincentives in future contracts of this type; i.e., when appropriate, obtain reasonable equitable adjustments to the contract as a remedy for subpar contractor performance. The Agency reported this recommendation as completed in MATS (appendix A, recommendation 2-1).

Fixed Air Monitoring Stations Contract Did Not Include Effective Disincentive

Of the three RadNet contracts, only the contract for fixed air monitoring stations contained incentives in the contract's Quality Assurance Surveillance Plan, as encouraged by FAR 16.401 and 16.403. Under the plan, the contractor had the potential to earn an additional $500 to $1,000 for making warranty repairs earlier than the 30 days required by the contract.

The performance standards in the Quality Assurance Surveillance Plan under the contract for fixed air monitoring stations listed a positive past performance evaluation as an incentive/disincentive. However, positive past performance evaluation is not a true incentive/disincentive, because performance evaluation is a FAR 42.15 requirement.

Even though the OIG raised the issue of disincentives in its January 2009 report, EPA did not add to the contract disincentives if the contractor made warranty repairs after the 30-day requirement. EPA did not effectively use disincentives. Under Delivery Orders 1 and 2, EPA had to extend the contractor period of performance to allow the contractor more time to deliver the required monitors. As a result, EPA received compensation valued at approximately $41,830 (appendix C). We do not consider this to be an effective disincentive because there were no enforceable contract requirements for EPA to receive compensation for untimely delivery.

Planned Disincentives Not Included in Spare Parts Contract

EPA did not include disincentives in the September 2010 RadNet spare parts contract. NAREL submitted a statement of work (SOW) for the spare parts contract to the OAM Procurement Operations Division in Research Triangle Park, which included discounts for untimely delivery. Specifically, the SOW included the following:

- Items shall be delivered within 90 days of order.
- Any item delivered after 90 days of order shall be invoiced at the following discount:
  - Delivery of any item between 91 and 120 days of order shall be invoiced with a discount of 2 percent.

> Delivery of any item after 120 days of order shall be invoiced with a discount of one additional percentage (1 percent) per additional 30-day delay.

However, none of the discounts outlined in the SOW were included in the awarded spare parts contract. The CO stated that the contract included terms for volume discounts, but the delivery discounts in the SOW were not included because the Procurement Operations Division decided to use a clause in the contract to allow the NAREL COR to determine delivery terms. However, the COR did not specify delivery terms to the contractor.

On March 9, 2011, EPA modified the contract to approve the 2011 price list. This modification included time frames for delivery, but still did not include any of the initial discounts outlined in the SOW for untimely delivery. Without using the types of disincentives outlined in the initial SOW, EPA has no readily quantifiable measure to hold the contractor accountable for timely completion of contract activities.

Installation of RadNet Monitors Behind Schedule

Contract oversight and contractor performance issues continue to hinder the delivery of RadNet monitors. As of November 30, 2011, EPA was 2 years and 5 months behind its initial schedule to install monitors established in the fixed air monitoring stations contract terms and conditions (table 7).

Table 7: Schedule of fixed air monitoring stations ordered and received

Delivery Order	Date awarded	Number ordered	Number delivered	Required start of delivery	Delivery order end date	EPA extended date for delivery	Date of last shipment	Late delivery timing
1	10/01/2007	51	51	01/31/2008	12/31/2008	04/30/2009	05/19/2009	4.6 months
2	06/10/2008	32	22	01/01/2009	07/31/2009	11/30/2011	07/08/2010	2 years, 5 months

Source: Delivery Orders 1 and 2, modifications, and OIG analysis.

Note: This contract was for 83 monitors, split between two delivery orders. The other 51 monitors were covered under an earlier contract. Per contract terms, the delivery and the ship dates are the same.

Delivery orders under the contract required the delivery of five monitoring stations per month beginning in January 2008. The OIG's January 2009 report recommended that the Agency track the installation of the RadNet system against the planned schedule in the CIPP until completed. The Agency has not reported this recommendation as completed in MATS; OAR recorded in MATS that it expected to complete monitor installation in spring 2011 (appendix A, recommendation 2-5). However, because of challenges brought on by the Japan nuclear incident, OAR now expects to complete installation of the remaining 10 monitors by June 2012.

EPA extended the period of performance for the delivery of the monitors to give the contractor additional time to deliver the required monitors. EPA extended Delivery Order 1 twice and Delivery Order 2 four times, with a final extension date of November 30, 2011, for Delivery Order 2.

EPA (figure 5, *left*) was responsible for installation delays, and the contractor (figure 5, *right*) was responsible for delivery delays.

Figure 5: Delays of delivery and installation of RadNet monitors

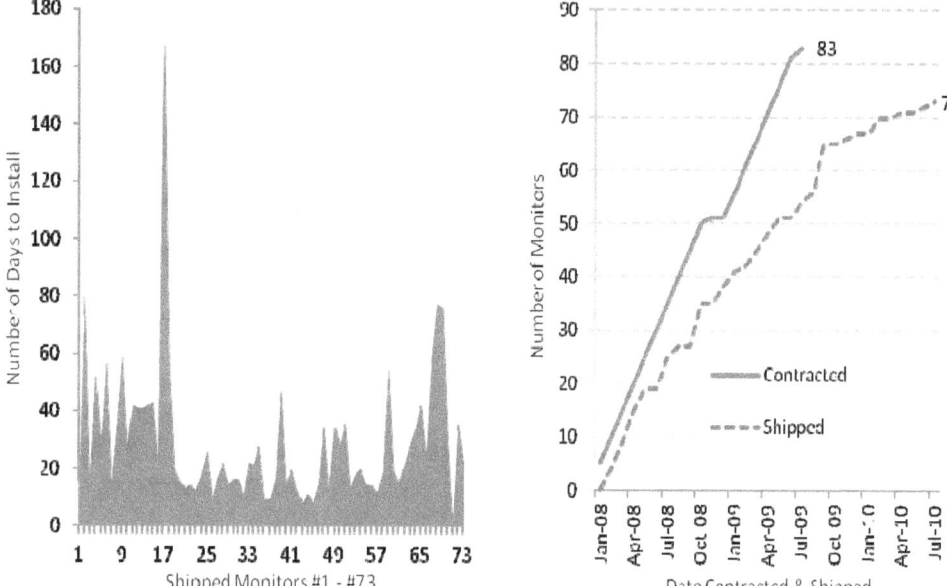

Source: OIG analysis of Delivery Orders 1 and 2, and EPA-provided data on shipment of monitors.

For EPA's part, NAREL was required to have five locations available per month for the contractor to deliver and install RadNet monitors at the required rate of five per month. However, the RadNet operations manager stated that he was unable to complete all the requirements at a rate of five locations per month, which delayed the delivery and installation of some of the monitors. Delivery and installation of RadNet monitoring stations by the contractor to a site requires NAREL to have identified sites and operators within cities designated by EPA, and to arrange for site preparation. To select operators, NAREL works with the EPA regions and departments of health in the states to find a volunteer to operate the monitor (i.e., change filters and submit data). Operators and state offices are not compensated. Site preparation may include installing electrical outlets, constructing mounting platforms, or erecting security fencing.

For the contractor's part, a subcontractor in Italy was unable to timely submit two proprietary components—local processor units and detectors. Further, in March 2011, EPA directed that components from the final 10 monitors under construction be used to fill a delivery order under the separate spare parts contract to provide parts needed to repair broken monitors that were already installed. This diversion of components away from construction of the final 10 monitors in Delivery Order 2 provided the spare parts contractor with enough equipment to repair the 25 monitors that were not working at the time of the Japan nuclear incident.

EPA is addressing the difficulty of acquiring proprietary spare parts with a foreign subcontractor by exploring domestic options. The December 2011 SOW for the newly awarded RadNet service contract[5] contains language to address the proprietary issue. For example, task 4 states:

> The contractor shall identify components that have or may develop limited availability or serviceability, and the contractor shall identify more readily available, improved or more serviceable components that may be potentially used to replace original components.

Monthly Progress Reports Not Effectively Used to Manage RadNet Contracts

EPA is not fully monitoring contractor performance through MPRs as required by FAR 42.11. Two of three RadNet contracts required MPRs; however, EPA required only one contractor to actually submit them (table 8).

Table 8: MPR requirements in the three RadNet contracts under review

Contract	MPR status
Fixed air monitoring stations	Required
Spare parts	Not required
Repair service	Required, but not enforced

Source: OIG analysis.

The OIG's January 2009 report recommended that the Agency use MPRs to monitor actual contractor performance against stated goals. The Agency reported this recommendation as completed in MATS (appendix A, recommendation 2-2).

The fixed air monitoring stations contract required the contractor to provide MPRs. NAREL received them as required, and they contained general information on contractor performance.

The spare parts contract did not include a requirement for MPRs; therefore, the contractor was not submitting them. Given this contractor's history of untimely delivery under the fixed air monitoring stations contract, EPA should have been monitoring the contractor's performance through MPRs.

---

[5] In the Agency response to the draft report, the Agency stated that the contract was awarded in December 2011.

The repair services contract included the following MPR requirement: "within the seven days of the end of each month, the Contractor shall provide a written report to the COR describing work performed during the month." However, the Agency did not require MPRs from the contractor. The COR stated that he required a repair report after each repair made, but did not require MPRs. As a result, EPA is not getting updated contractor activity as required, and documented contractor performance information is not available for use in contractor performance evaluations.

Contractor Performance Evaluations Not Timely or Completed

As of October 12, 2011, EPA had not timely completed four of five required contractor performance evaluations for the RadNet contractors. The OIG's January 2009 report recommended that the CO and COR formally evaluate the fixed air monitoring station contractor's performance on an annual basis and enter past performance information into the NIH CPS under the expired and current contract. The Agency reported this recommendation as completed in MATS (appendix A, recommendation 2-3).

To ensure compliance with FAR 42.15, COs were required to include EPAAR Clause 1552.209-76 in their contracts, which requires annual contractor performance evaluations. Effective May 15, 2010, EPAAR Deviation 1542.15 replaced EPAAR 1509.170, to require the entry of the contractor evaluations into PPIRS instead of NIH CPS. Contractor performance evaluations in PPIRS are available to all federal contracting offices nationwide.

Contractor past performance is one of many factors to consider when assessing whether contractors are likely to be successful in controlling contract costs and meeting contract expectations. When EPA documents evaluations in an untimely manner or not at all, selection teams within EPA and at other federal agencies do not have current contractor evaluation information to consider when making new contract awards.

As of October 12, 2011, EPA should have performed five contractor performance evaluations: three for the fixed air monitoring stations contract and two for the repair services contract.[6] However, only one for the fixed air monitoring stations contract was completed (table 9).

---

[6] The spare parts contractor performance evaluation was not due until after our review period ended. The contract was awarded in September 2010; the evaluation period covers 1 year and is due 90 days after the evaluation period ends.

Table 9: Timeliness of contractor performance evaluations

Contract	Required period	Date due	Completed	Period covered	Days past due as of 10/12/2011
EP-W-07-076 Fixed Air Monitoring Stations	09/28/07–09/27/08	02/12/09	01/30/09	09/27/07–12/30/08[a]	N/A
	09/28/08–09/27/09	02/11/10	No	N/A	420
	09/28/09–09/27/10	02/13/11	No	N/A	168
EP-D-08-068 Repair Services	05/12/08–05/11/09	09/24/09	No	N/A	513
	05/12/08–05/11/10	09/24/10	No	N/A	262

Source: OIG analysis of contractor performance evaluations as of October 12, 2011.

[a] The initial evaluation improperly covered 15 months; the regulation requires the evaluation to cover a maximum period of 12 months.

The CO for the fixed air monitoring stations contract stated that conducting the contractor evaluation was not a priority. Further, during the transition from the NIH CPS system to CPARS/PPIRS, the COs had only limited access to CPARS, yet were required to enter more data than was previously required.

EPA conducted none of the required evaluations for the repair services contract, and the requirements for evaluations were not included in the terms and conditions of the contract. The CO stated that he would conduct the evaluation on close-out of the contract. In May 2009, the COR reminded the CO to complete the required performance evaluation. However, as of October 12, 2011, none of the required performance evaluations had been conducted.

Conclusion

OAM and OAR did not adequately oversee the three RadNet contracts we reviewed and did not fully use contract requirements, including using contract incentives and disincentives, MPRs, and annual performance evaluations, to hold contractors accountable. As a result, contract issues raised in our January 2009 report continue to exist because EPA believed it could oversee and hold contractors accountable without them. EPA should implement recommended actions from this report to hold RadNet contractors accountable. Doing so will help ensure that EPA's network of monitors is fully installed and operational so it can meet requirements established in the National Response Framework for Nuclear Radiological Incidents.

Recommendations

We recommend that the Assistant Administrator for Air and Radiation, in conjunction with the Assistant Administrator for Administration and Resources Management:

4. Require follow-on RadNet contracts to include incentives/disincentives and a requirement for MPRs.

5. Require the CO and COR to formally evaluate RadNet contractors' performance on an annual basis and enter information into PPIRS through CPARS.

6. Determine whether domestic contract options are available for crucial repair parts that are identified as only being available from a foreign subcontractor.

7. Review the information in MATS for the prior audit and ensure it is accurate and current.

We recommend that the Assistant Administrator for Air and Radiation:

8. Track the installation of the RadNet monitors against the revised schedule and use the contract requirements in recommendations 4 and 5 to hold the contractor accountable.

Agency Response and OIG Evaluation

The Agency generally concurred with the findings and recommendations, and provided milestone dates for most of the proposed corrective actions. The Agency also proposed some revised language, which we incorporated where appropriate in the report. The Agency's full response is in appendix D.

The Agency partially concurred with recommendation 4 to require that RadNet contracts include incentives/disincentives and require MPRs for follow-on contracts, but not for existing contracts. We agree with the Agency corrective action for recommendation 4 and have revised the recommendation. We request that the Agency provide the awarded contract and statement of work for contract EP-D-12-003 and the follow-on contract EP-D-10-0085 as soon as the information becomes a available.

The Agency partially agreed with recommendation 5 to require the CO and COR to formally evaluate RadNet contractors' performance on an annual basis. The Agency stated that it will track and report timely completion of contractor performance evaluations under a Balanced Scorecard Internal Business Performance Measure and that new and/or ongoing contracts will receive priority for completing past performance reporting over expired contracts. The Agency further stated that a target of not less than 90 percent of past performance evaluations is to be completed in CPARS and contractor performance evaluations will be brought up to date as applicable. We continue to recommend that EPA formally evaluate RadNet contractors' performance, even if the contract has expired, and enter information into PPIRS through CPARS. FAR does not make exceptions for contractor evaluation based on whether contracts are active or expired. We request that the Agency include a date for doing so in the 90-day response to the final report.

The Agency agreed with recommendation 6 and stated that it is conducting additional market research in accordance with FAR Part 10 to identify potential domestic sources prior to the re-compete of the spare parts contract. This contract is anticipated to be awarded prior to the end of fiscal year 2012. We agree with the Agency corrective action for recommendation 6.

The Agency agreed with recommendation 7 and provided the status of recommendations from OIG Report No. 09-P-0087. We agree with the Agency corrective action for recommendation 7 and request that the Agency include information on the finalized February and April 2012 performance evaluations under contract EP-W-07-076 in the 90-day response to the final report.

The Agency concurred with recommendation 8 and stated that the COR is working with the CO to enforce the terms and conditions of the contract including receipt of consideration for late deliveries. We agree with the Agency corrective plan for recommendation 8. However, since the expected completion date of installation of monitors is now June 2012, we request that the Agency include information in the 90-day response to the final report on any consideration the Agency received for the additional delayed delivery of the monitors.

Status of Recommendations and Potential Monetary Benefits

		RECOMMENDATIONS				POTENTIAL MONETARY BENEFIT (in $000s)	
Rec. No.	Page No.	Subject	Status[1]	Action Official	Planned Completion Date	Claimed Amount	Agreed-To Amount
1	14	Establish and enforce written expectations for RadNet operational readiness commensurate with its role and importance to EPA's mission. Include, at a minimum:	O	Assistant Administrator for Air and Radiation	04/01/12		
		a. Percentage of stationary monitors expected to be operational.					
		b. Maximum length of time stationary monitors are permitted to be nonoperational.					
		c. Plan for temporarily backing up broken stationary monitors when operational status is lower than required.					
		d. Availability of monitor operators.					
2	14	Implement metrics for RadNet operational readiness to be reviewed daily by NAREL, and periodically by OAR (at least monthly) and by the Deputy Administrator (as needed), to include, at a minimum:	O	Assistant Administrator for Air and Radiation	04/01/12		
		a. Percentage of monitors operational.					
		b. Length of time in nonoperational status.					
		c. Need for backup monitors when operational status is too low.					
		d. Operator availability.					
3	14	Direct that NAREL improve planning and management for RadNet to include, at a minimum:		Assistant Administrator for Air and Radiation			
		a. Provide for in-stock spare parts to assure operational status established under recommendation 1.	O		04/09/12		
		b. Implement measures to assure that operators are available.	O		04/01/12		
		c. How often filter changes are needed to provide consistency in throughput at NAREL's analytical laboratory and implement a metric for these filter changes.	U				
4	24	Require follow-on RadNet contracts to include incentives/disincentives and a requirement for MPRs.	O	Assistant Administrator for Air and Radiation, in conjunction with the Assistant Administrator for Administration and Resources Management	9/30/12		

RECOMMENDATIONS

Rec. No.	Page No.	Subject	Status[1]	Action Official	Planned Completion Date	Claimed Amount	Agreed-To Amount
5	24	Require the CO and COR to formally evaluate RadNet contractors' performance on an annual basis and enter information into PPIRS through CPARS.	U	Assistant Administrator for Air and Radiation, in conjunction with the Assistant Administrator for Administration and Resources Management			
6	24	Determine whether domestic contract options are available for crucial repair parts that are identified as only being available from a foreign subcontractor.	O	Assistant Administrator for Air and Radiation, in conjunction with the Assistant Administrator for Administration and Resources Management	09/30/12		
7	24	Review the information in MATS for the prior audit and ensure it is accurate and current.	O	Assistant Administrator for Air and Radiation, in conjunction with the Assistant Administrator for Administration and Resources Management	06/30/12		
8	24	Track the installation of the RadNet monitors against the revised schedule and use contract requirements in recommendations 4 and 5 to hold the contractor accountable.	O	Assistant Administrator for Air and Radiation	06/30/12		

[1] O = recommendation is open with agreed-to corrective actions pending
C = recommendation is closed with all agreed-to actions completed
U = recommendation is unresolved with resolution efforts in progress

Analysis of Prior EPA OIG Report Recommendations

#	OIG recommendations	Information from MATS		OIG analysis
		Completed	Actions taken	
2-1	Maintain current incentives in the new RadNet contract and seek opportunities to expand these and include disincentives in future contracts of this type. When appropriate, obtain reasonable equitable adjustments to the contract as a remedy for subpar contractor performance.	2009-01-30	The COR is evaluating contractor performance on a monthly basis for potential subpar performance by methods described in 2-2. If subpar performance is identified, the CO will seek reasonable equitable adjustment to the contract as a remedy.	Not complete
2-2	Use the monthly progress reports to monitor actual contractor performance against stated goals.	2009-01-30	The COR is conducting weekly scheduled telephone meetings and will discuss any discrepancies between actual performance and stated goals with the contractor. These discrepancies will be reported to the CO. The COR is receiving monthly progress reports with clear description of contracted and actual delivery dates.	Not complete
2-3	Require the CO and COR to formally evaluate the contractor's performance on an annual basis and enter past performance information into the National Institutes of Health's (NIH's) Contractor Performance System under the expired and current contract.	2008-04-24	We completed the contractor performance evaluation for expired contract and delivery order and submitted it to the CO on April 24, 2008, for entry into NIH's Contractor Performance System.	Not complete
		2009-01-30	Contractor performance evaluation for the current contract and its first delivery order is currently in progress and we will submit it to the CO for entry into NIH's system by January 30, 2009 (30 days after delivery order due date)	
2-4	Establish a plan, with milestone dates, for completing the SAB recommended testing and, if needed, develop and implement a plan for making design improvements.	2009-07-30	Issue report with evaluation of test data and recommendations on design changes. The report did not recommend any design changes.	Complete

#	OIG recommendations	Information from MATS		OIG analysis
		Completed	Actions taken	
2-5	Monitor the upgrade of the RadNet system against the planned schedule in the CIPP until completed.	Not completed	OAR originally expected to complete the installation of monitors in the spring 2011. However, because of challenges brought on by the Japan incident, OAR now expects to complete installation of the monitors by the end of 2011. The network will include a total of 134 monitors. The reduction in the total number of monitors purchased is due to budget reductions as well as meeting our long-term performance target of monitors within the 100 most populous cities. In addition, with 134 monitors we also meet our long-term goal of population coverage within 25 miles of a monitor (55%). Final corrective action for this review will be completed by September 30, 2012.	Not completed

Source: EPA-reported information from MATS.

Analysis of 25 Out-of-Service Monitors as of March 11, 2011—Date of Japan Nuclear Incident

Monitor No.	Monitor location	Date out of service	Notification date[a]	Days to notification	Date back in service	Days out of service
EPA was unable to provide government-furnished parts						
1	Harlingen, TX	01/28/10	03/25/11	421	04/01/11	428
2	Raleigh, NC	03/29/10	03/26/11	362	04/08/11	375
3	Fort Wayne, IN	05/02/10	03/20/11	322	03/25/11	327
4	St. Louis, MO	06/09/10	03/19/11	283	03/30/11	294
5	Oklahoma City, OK	10/17/10	03/19/11	153	03/24/11	158
6	Burlington, VT	11/02/10	03/20/11	138	03/28/11	146
7	Fort Smith, AR	11/06/10	03/24/11	138	03/31/11	145
8	San Diego, CA	10/26/10	02/23/11	120	03/20/11	145
9	St. Paul, MN	11/08/10	01/12/11	65	03/31/11	143
10	Philadelphia, PA	12/28/10	01/12/11	15	03/14/11	76
11	Hartford, CT	12/29/10	01/13/11	15	03/11/11	72
12	Lubbock, TX	01/22/11	02/23/11	32	03/30/11	67
13	Syracuse, NY	01/23/11	03/20/11	56	03/18/11	54
14	Chicago, IL	02/02/11	03/20/11	46	03/22/11	48
15	Milwaukee, WI	02/05/11	03/20/11	43	03/24/11	47
16	El Paso, TX	02/09/11	02/23/11	14	03/28/11	47
17	Phoenix, AZ	02/11/11	02/23/11	12	03/24/11	41
18	Buffalo, NY	02/19/11	03/25/11	34	03/30/11	39
19	Fontana, CA	02/11/11	02/23/11	12	03/21/11	38
20	Reno, NV	02/19/11	03/19/11	28	03/24/11	33
21	Memphis, TN	03/05/11	03/25/11	20	03/31/11	26
22	Laredo, TX	03/04/11	N/A[b]	-	03/15/11	11
No operator						
23	Carlsbad, NM	06/01/10	N/A	N/A	03/24/11	296
24	Corpus Christi, TX	10/01/10	N/A	N/A	03/21/11	171
A definite "out-of-service" date not easily defined; monitor running erratically/intermittently						
25	Yuma, AZ	02/25/11	02/23/11[c]	-2	03/17/11	20
Average days to notify service contractor:				106		
Average days out of service:						130

Source: OIG analysis of 25 out-of-service monitors per information provided by EPA.
[a] Date that EPA notified the contractor that the monitor was out of service.
[b] No notification went out. On March 4, 2011, the operations manager and the operator began troubleshooting the problem, which resulted in the return to service on March 15, 2011.
[c] EPA notified the contractor by phone 2 days earlier than the officially recorded out-of-service date.

Extensions to the Fixed Air Monitoring Stations Contract and EPA Compensation Received

Modifi-cation No.	Extended date for delivery of monitor	Purpose of extension	Value of compen-sation	Actual compensation received
Delivery Order 1—period of performance: 10/01/07 to 12/31/08 $3,011,902 paid to contractor as of 09/01/2011				
2	02/27/2009	Delivery and installation of monitors	$14,200	Upgrade to front end software
3	04/30/2009	Delivery and installation of monitors	N/A	Warranties for nine monitors extended from 12 months to 18 months
4	04/30/2009	Extend the date for completion of warranty repairs for five defective monitors	$14,416	Provide two MAB units and a 12-hour "test run" for each new monitor
Delivery Order 2—period of performance: 01/01/09 to 07/31/09 $1,457,804 paid to contractor as of 09/01/2011				
1	10/30/2009	Delivery delays from a subcontractor of LPUs and detectors	$13,187	Repair/replacement of the gamma detector of the monitor located at NAREL
3	10/30/2010	EPA unable to provide all delivery addresses to the contractor	N/A	N/A
4	04/30/2011	Excusable delays clause—fire destroyed a subcontractor facility	N/A	N/A
5	11/30/2011	Provide time for the contractor to reconstruct the final 10 monitors	N/A	N/A
Total EPA compensation received			$41,803	

Source: Modifications to Delivery Orders 1 and 2 of the fixed air monitoring stations contract and OIG analysis.

Agency Response to Draft Report

UNITED STATES ENVIRONMENTAL PROTECTION AGENCY
WASHINGTON, D.C. 20460

February 3, 2012

MEMORANDUM

SUBJECT: Response to OIG Draft Project Report No. OA-FY11-0184

FROM: Gina McCarthy, Assistant Administrator
Office of Air and Radiation

Craig Hooks, Assistant Administrator
Office of Administration and Resource Management

TO: Melissa M. Heist, Assistant Inspector General for Audit
Office of the Inspector General

This memorandum is in response to the Office of Inspector General's (OIG's) request for comments on the draft project report dated December 15, 2011: *Weaknesses in EPA's Management of the Radiation Network System Demand Attention.*

As requested by the OIG, the Office of Air and Radiation (OAR) and the Office of Administration and Resource Management (OARM) and transmit the Agency's consolidated response to this report as an attachment to this memorandum.

While we agree with most of the proposed recommendations, we have identified some revisions in the draft report, as well as some suggested language to assist the OIG in their final report. Per your request, we are also providing planned completion dates for all agreed-to recommendations.

 Please feel free contact us directly, or your staff may contact Jonathan Edwards, at (202) 343-9437, if you have any questions.

Attachment

cc: Mike Davis

RESPONSE TO OIG DRAFT REPORT (Project No. OA-FY11-0184)

This response is organized into two main sections. The first section combines all of the draft report's recommendations and related responses. The second section provides the EPA's other comments which focus largely on contract matters, sampling frequency and filter changes and their relationship to data quality, and the RadNet's Quality Assurance Manual and Quality Assurance Project Plan. In many cases, the EPA comments are accompanied by suggested revisions to clarify perceived misunderstandings or to correct inaccuracies. The EPA is particularly concerned about the statements concerning "relaxed quality controls" since the EPA contends that this is inaccurate, as described in detail in the appropriate places in this response. For convenience, red text is used to indicate some suggested revisions.

Responses to OIG Recommendations

Recommendation 1a: *Establish and enforce written expectations for RadNet operational readiness commensurate with its role in and importance to EPA's mission. Include, at a minimum: Percentage of stationary monitors expected to be operational.*

> **Response:** The EPA concurs and has been reevaluating its current operational goal, and will finalize this effort by April 1, 2012.

Recommendation 1b: *Establish and enforce written expectations for RadNet operational readiness commensurate with its role in and importance to EPA's mission. Include, at a minimum: Maximum length of time stationary monitors are permitted to be nonoperational.*

> **Response:** EPA concurs and has established a maximum length of time for RadNet fixed monitors to be nonoperational before reporting to ORIA and OAR management, along with a process for evaluating and reporting the circumstances associated with the nonoperational status. The reporting requirement will begin April 1, 2012.

Recommendation 1c: *Establish and enforce written expectations for RadNet operational readiness commensurate with its role in and importance to EPA's mission. Include, at a minimum: Plan for temporarily backing up broken stationary monitors when operational status is lower than required.*

> **Response:** EPA concurs and has evaluated various options for backing up broken stationary monitors, and will complete the written documentation and plan by April 1, 2012.

Recommendation 1d: *Establish and enforce written expectations for RadNet operational readiness commensurate with its role in and importance to EPA's mission. Include, at a minimum: Availability of monitor operators.*

> **Response:** EPA concurs with the importance of monitor operator availability and will finalize written plans for maximizing operator availability by April 1, 2012. However, EPA cannot assign volunteers or enforce expectations upon them. Instead, EPA seeks

volunteers, without compensation, for their time and effort. RadNet personnel work closely with their partners, particularly the EPA regions, to do their best in recruiting volunteer operators. When a suitable volunteer operator is identified, EPA also requests a backup volunteer who works with the primary operator to maximize operator availability. Most locations have a backup operator identified and fully trained in all aspects of monitor operations. Once EPA finds an operator, the RadNet volunteer coordinator provides information to them routinely and is in frequent contact by phone. EPA also provides recognition, such as letters of appreciation to their supervisors, for their service in an effort to maintain a good relationship with our volunteers. The response to recommendation 2d contains provisions for reporting to senior EPA management when operators are unavailable for an extended period of time.

Recommendation 2a: *Implement metrics for RadNet operational readiness to be reviewed daily by NAREL, and periodically by OAR (at least monthly) and by the Deputy Administrator (at least quarterly), to include, at a minimum: Percentage of monitors operational.*

> **Response:** EPA concurs with the importance of maintaining operational readiness metrics. NAREL will continue to monitor, measure and review RadNet operational readiness every business day. The percentage of operating monitors will be included in written reports, developed using the following process:
> - weekly reports on metrics for ORIA;
> - monthly status summary reports for review by ORIA and OAR management; and
> - OAR management will advise the Deputy Administrator, when deemed appropriate,
>
> This reporting process will be established and begin April 1, 2012.

Recommendation 2b: *Implement metrics for RadNet operational readiness to be reviewed daily by NAREL, and periodically by OAR (at least monthly) and by the Deputy Administrator (at least quarterly), to include, at a minimum: Length of time in nonoperational status.*

> **Response:** EPA concurs with the importance of maintaining operational readiness metrics. The reports described in response to recommendation 2a will include a list of the operational status of all monitors, along with the repair status and anticipated date for non-operational monitors to return to service. This reporting process will be established and begin April 1, 2012.

Recommendation 2c: *Implement metrics for RadNet operational readiness to be reviewed daily by NAREL, and periodically by OAR (at least monthly) and by the Deputy Administrator (at least quarterly), to include, at a minimum: Need for backup monitors when operational status is too low.*

> **Response:** EPA concurs with the importance of maintaining operational readiness. This expectation is being met through the repair of out-of-service monitors. The reports described in response to recommendation 2a will be informed by the evaluation of options for backing up broken monitors, as described in response to recommendation 1c. This reporting process will be established and begin April 1, 2012.

Recommendation 2d: *Implement metrics for RadNet operational readiness to be reviewed daily by NAREL, and periodically by OAR (at least monthly) and by the Deputy Administrator (at least quarterly), to include, at a minimum: Operator availability.*

> **Response:** EPA concurs with the importance of maintaining operational readiness metrics. This information will be included in the monthly reports described in 2a. This information will also be forwarded to the appropriate EPA Regional Radiation Managers. This process will be established and begin April 1, 2012.

Recommendation 2e: *Implement metrics for RadNet operational readiness to be reviewed daily by NAREL, and periodically by OAR (at least monthly) and by the Deputy Administrator (at least quarterly), to include, at a minimum: Frequency of filter changes per the QAM and QAPP.*

> **Response:** EPA concurs with the importance of operational readiness metrics. However, the frequency of filter changes is not a relevant metric for operational readiness. For clarification, the Quality Assurance Manual (QAM) described in the draft OIG report does not apply to the RadNet fixed real-time monitors; it explicitly excludes them, and notes that the routine operations Quality Assurance Project Plan (QAPP) for RadNet real-time monitors is the applicable quality document. Also for clarification, the twice weekly filter change references in this QAPP are intended to provide consistency in throughput at NAREL's analytical laboratory, not as an operational requirement. The QAPP for RadNet real-time monitors has been edited to clarify this intent.

Recommendation 3a: *Direct that NAREL improve planning and management for RadNet to include, at a minimum: Provide for in-stock spare parts to assure operational status established under recommendation 1.*

> **Response:** EPA concurs and the corrective action has been completed. The spare parts contract is now in place, there is an inventory of spare parts, and funding is budgeted for additional inventory of proprietary spare parts. Funding for spare parts for future years is also included in NAREL's projected long-term RadNet budget. This is based upon repair rates to date coupled with aging of the monitors. Additionally, NAREL is pursuing the required funding to have the repair contractor investigate lower cost/higher availability spare parts that can replace the proprietary spare parts.

Recommendation 3b: *Direct that NAREL improve planning and management for RadNet to include, at a minimum: Implement measures to assure that operators are available.*

> **Response:** EPA concurs with the importance of maximizing operator availability and will explore measures by April 1, 2012. However, EPA cannot assign volunteer operators or enforce availability of volunteer operators. Instead, EPA seeks volunteers, without compensation, for their time and effort. RadNet personnel work closely with their partners, particularly the EPA regions, to recruit volunteer operators. When a suitable volunteer operator is identified, EPA also requests a backup volunteer who works with the primary operator to maximize operator availability. Most locations have a backup

operator identified and fully trained in all aspects of monitor operations. Once EPA finds an operator, the RadNet volunteer coordinator provides information to them routinely and is in frequent contact by phone. EPA also provides recognition, such as letters of appreciation to their supervisors, for their service in an effort to maintain a good relationship with our volunteers. The response to recommendation 2d contains provisions for reporting to senior EPA management when operators are unavailable for an extended period of time.

Recommendation 4: *Modify existing and require follow-on RadNet contracts to include incentives/disincentives and a requirement for* Monthly Performance Reviews *(MPRs).*

Response: EPA concurs with the draft report findings pertaining to **EP-W-07-076** for Fixed Air Monitoring Stations. As this contract ends on March 31, 2012 (Delivery Order 3), there is no meaningful performance period remaining against which to apply the recommendation under the existing contract.

EPA also concurs with the draft report findings pertaining to **EP-D-08-068** for repair and maintenance services. However this contract has expired, and follow-on contract **EP-D-12-003,** awarded on December 12, 2011, for RadNet Air Maintenance, includes detailed performance metrics and provides for a deduction in the invoiced amount for failure to meet those targets. Contract **EP-D-12-003** also contains detailed invoice reporting requirements which duplicate the information included in an MPR, thereby satisfying the recommendation.

With respect to contract **EP-D-10-0085,** again the EPA concurs with draft report findings. The follow-on contract is currently in the planning stages for award prior to the end of FY 2012. The resultant contract will include appropriate incentives, quality control requirements, and reporting requirements consistent with this recommendation.

Recommendation 5: *Require the CO and COR to formally evaluate RadNet contractors' performance on an annual basis and enter information into PPIRS through CPARS.*

Response: The EPA will track and report timely completion of contractor performance evaluations under a Balanced Scorecard Internal Business Performance Measure. This will require 100% of contracts eligible to be entered into CPARS during the fiscal year, and a target of not less than 90% of past performance evaluations to be accomplished in CPARS within timeframes required in the Federal Acquisition Regulation (FAR). Accordingly, new and/or ongoing contracts will receive priority for completing past performance reporting over expired contracts, although contractor performance evaluations will be brought up to date as applicable.

Recommendation 6: *Determine whether domestic contract options are available for crucial repair parts that are identified as only being available from a foreign subcontractor.*

Response: The EPA is conducting additional market research in accordance with FAR Part 10 to identify potential domestic sources prior to the re-compete of the spare parts contract. This contract is anticipated to be awarded prior to the end of FY 2012.

Recommendation 7: *Review the information in MATS for OIG Report No. 09-P-0087 and ensure it is accurate and current.*

Response: OIG Report No. 09-P-0087 contained findings and recommendations on several OAM contracts/orders. Below is the status on those past performance reporting requirements identified in MATS, as well as the RadNet delivery schedule.

- Past performance evaluations for EP-W-05-012 were finalized in the system on 1/30/2009.
- Past performance evaluations for 2008 and 2009 for Delivery Order 2 under EP-W-07-076 were finalized in the system on 1/30/2009.
- The 2010 past performance evaluation for Delivery Order 2 under EP-W-07-076 was finalized on 2/3/2012.
- The past performance evaluation for Delivery Order 3 under EP-W-07-076 will be entered in April 2012 when the order has ended.
- The expected completion date of installation or receipt of monitors is June 2012.

Recommendation 8: *Track the installation of the RadNet monitors against the revised schedule and use the contract requirements in recommendations 4 and 5 to hold the contractor accountable.*

Response: EPA concurs and the COR is working with the CO to enforce the terms and conditions of the contract including receipt of consideration for late deliveries.

Comments on Text of Draft Report other than the Recommendations

Pg. 3, Par. 2 and Table 1

The sentence just prior to Table 1 states that the contract for spare parts was awarded to the same contractor as for purchasing fixed monitors. While this is accurate, the EPA believes it is important to note that this was done for proprietary spare parts only, since there is no other known option. Currently, the proprietary parts are required for proper operation of the monitor. The EPA suggests the sentence read, "The contracts for fixed air monitoring stations and spare parts were awarded to the same contractor due to the proprietary nature of those spare parts."

In Table 1, the total contract obligations under RadNet contract EP-D-10-085 for spare parts should be $1,405,913.29, in lieu of $8,517,587.00 as follows:

Contract	Delivery Order	Date	Amount
EP-D-10-085	0001	September 21, 2010	$279,415.29
EP-D-10-085	0002	March 9, 2011	$127,495.00
EP-D-10-085	0003	March 19, 2011	$503,619.00
EP-D-10-085	0004	June 3, 2011	$495,384.00
			$1,405,913.29

Pg. 3, Last Par.

The second sentence says that the EPA increased sampling frequency following the Japanese nuclear incidents. For clarification, the EPA suggests that the sentence be revised to read, "In response to the Japan nuclear incident, the EPA increased sampling frequency for the milk and drinking water networks and increased analysis frequency for all networks to detect and measure radiation levels, and inform the public of any changes in those levels."

Pg. 7, Par. 1

Since most of the late filter changes cited in this paragraph occurred while monitors were inoperable, EPA suggests that this fact be noted in the paragraph.

Moreover, for an operating RadNet real-time monitor, reduced frequency of filter changes does not adversely affect either the hourly gamma data or their availability– nor does it adversely affect the gamma data obtained from laboratory analysis.

One of the documents cited as containing filter change frequency is the 2008 RadNet Quality Assurance Manual (QAM). To clarify, this QAM does not describe operations or requirements of the RadNet real-time monitors that are the subject of this report; Section 5.3.4.1 of the QAM notes that the QAPP (for RadNet real-time monitors) is the applicable quality document for routine operations, not the QAM: "5.3.4.1 The RadNet air particulate monitoring program is currently undergoing an expansion and upgrade to include near real-time gamma monitors. This long-term project of installing additional monitors began in 2006 and will not near completion until 2009. Please refer to the *NAREL Quality Assurance Project Plan for Expansion of the RadNet Fixed Station Air Monitoring System to Include Near Real-Time Gamma Monitoring* (RadNet/QAPP-1) for information. This manual [QAM] addresses all other aspects of the RadNet air monitoring program." EPA suggests that this QAM reference be deleted as a document associated with these monitors.

Finally, for clarification, the twice weekly filter change references in the QAPP are intended to provide consistency in throughput at NAREL's analytical laboratory, not as operational requirements.

As noted in the QAPP in sections 2.0 (page 14) and 7.0 (page 25), there is a distinct difference between the RadNet real-time and RadNet legacy (described in the QAM) monitors and the use of their filters. The filters from the RadNet real-time monitors actually measure radiation emitted from the filters themselves, and the monitors report the results continuously. In contrast, the filters from RadNet legacy monitors are the only way in which sampling/data can be collected from them. While filters from both types of monitors are sent to the analytical laboratory for analysis, the frequency of filter change for the RadNet real-time monitor does not affect the quality of the results from either the real-time data (from the filters) or the laboratory analysis of the filters.

Suggested Revision: Pg. 7, Par. 1

Broken RadNet monitors and resulting late filter changes may impair this critical infrastructure asset. On March 11, 2011, at the time of the Japan nuclear incident emergency, 25 of the 124 installed RadNet monitors, or 20 percent, were out of service for an average of 130 days. In addition, 6 of the 12 RadNet monitors we sampled (50 percent) had gone over 8 weeks without a filter change, and 2 had gone unchanged for over 300 days because these monitors were broken. Unless EPA grants an extension, the repair services contract requires a service contractor to fix broken monitors within 14 days of EPA's notification that a monitor is out of service. The EPA QAPP refers to operators changing filters on fixed RadNet real-time monitors twice a week. Because EPA did not manage RadNet as a high-priority program this resulted in parts shortages, insufficient contract oversight, and contributed to the extensive delay in fixing broken monitors. In addition, broken RadNet real-time monitors and relaxed quality controls contributed to the filters not being changed timely. Out-of-service monitors and unchanged filters may reduce the availability and quality of critical data. As a result, EPA may not have sufficient data to determine levels of airborne radioactivity and the associated threat to public health and the environment

EPA recognizes the expressed concern about RadNet station operability, and we have taken steps to address the issue more completely; however, the RadNet system was able to provide sufficient data to determine levels of airborne radioactivity during the weeks after the Fukushima nuclear power plant incident. EPA worked very closely with the interagency scientific and public health communities during the Fukushima response to properly characterize our findings and in the development of our public messages.

Pg. 7, Par. 2 and Par. 3

As another point of clarification, filter changes for RadNet monitors are requested at a rate of twice per week for consistency with the legacy air monitoring program and for NAREL's analytical laboratory work load planning purposes. As previously stated, the referenced QAM is not applicable to the RadNet real-time monitoring network. Twice weekly filter changes are not required for RadNet real-time monitors because changing filters less than twice weekly does not adversely affect data quality or availability.

EPA also notes again that the spare parts contract is with the same contractor which makes the monitor. This is solely for procuring proprietary parts that are not available through other vendors.

EPA suggests minor wording changes to clarify these points in the following paragraphs in redline-strikeout format.

Suggested Revision: Pg. 7, Par. 2

EPA included terms and conditions in the RadNet repair and maintenance services contract to define the period of time for repair., and EPA established quality control standards for frequency of filter changes. In May 2008, EPA awarded a RadNet repair and maintenance service contract that requires the contractor to fix broken monitors within 14 days of being notified by the COR. EPA may permit an extension of this 14-day period for a specific repair for reasons including unavailability of government-furnished equipment, operator unavailability, and physical disruption of the site. EPA acquires the GFP from the contractor that was awarded through the proprietary spare parts contract.

Suggested Revision: Pg. 7, Par. 3

For laboratory workload planning, EPA's QAM and QAPP estimates that, under routine circumstances, RadNet air station operators collect air particulate filters twice a week and mail the filters via the U.S. Postal Service to NAREL for analysis. When elevated levels of radioactivity are anticipated or known to exist, EPA may request RadNet station operators to increase the sampling frequency and use priority shipping.

Pg. 9, Par. 1

The first paragraph on page 9 contains the sentences "EPA did not have the required parts to provide to the repair contractor, and would not for an extended period of time. Therefore, EPA did not notify the contractor that these monitors were in need of repair." EPA agrees with these sentences, and suggests that similar sentences be included in the last paragraph on page 9 for completeness to indicate why the COR took 120 to 421 days to notify the repair contractor.

Pg. 9, Par. 2

In the second paragraph on page 9, the phrase "had not assigned operators for two monitors" is used. Since EPA cannot assign operators, we suggest that the phrase "had not been able to recruit replacement volunteer operators" be used instead.

Pg. 10, Par. 1

EPA requests the first sentence on page 10 be revised to indicate that some repair requests had been made to the service contractor prior to the earthquake, and that the priority repairs were made possible only by "cannibalizing" monitors in the process of being constructed. EPA suggests the first paragraph on page 10 be changed to read (changes highlighted in red):

<u>Suggested Revision: Pg. 10, Par. 1</u>
"Eighteen of the 25 out-of-service monitors received EPA's priority attention only after the Japan nuclear incident. Although 7 out-of-service monitors had been scheduled for repair prior to the Japan incident, the remaining 18 out-of-service monitors received EPA's priority attention only after the incident The priority attention consisted of cannibalizing monitors under construction for their parts which were used to repair broken monitors. By April 8, 2011, the service contractor had completed repairs on all monitors (figure 4)."

Pg. 11, Par. 2

Since the QAM is not an applicable reference for the RadNet real time monitors, EPA suggests removing references to it in the first sentence of this paragraph and the preceding bullets. Also, the context of the QAPP section referenced (laboratory analytical scheduling) should be noted in this sentence. EPA suggests the sentence read "The RadNet QAPP estimates twice-a-week filter changes for laboratory analytical scheduling purposes."

Pg. 11, Last Par

In the last paragraph on page 11, EPA recommends removing the statement that there is a requirement to change filters twice per week. Since changing filters less frequently than twice per week does not affect hourly gamma data quality or availability or laboratory analysis for gamma radiation, this does not adversely affect data completeness and does not potentially impair RadNet's ability to protect public health. EPA suggests the last paragraph on page 11 read as follows (changes highlighted in red).

<u>Suggested Revision: Pg. 11, Par. 2</u>

Further, NAREL gave operators permission to wait up to 8 days between filter changes, despite the requirement to change the filters initial provisional request of twice a week in the QAM and QAPP. Some operators requested and NAREL gave permission to change filters once a week. Failure to follow RadNet quality assurance requirements may adversely affect data completeness and potentially impairs RadNet's ability to protect human health

Pg. 12, Par. 2

The second paragraph of page 12 is correct. For clarification however, EPA requests that language be added to clarify that, even though there was not a spare parts contract in place, EPA was purchasing proprietary spare parts from the vendor using individual purchase orders. EPA suggests the following language be added to the end of this paragraph to reflect this: "Prior to award of the Spare Parts Contract, multiple stand-alone purchase orders totaling over $200,000 were placed with the manufacturer for proprietary parts not available from other vendors. These various orders included computers (LPU's), detector assemblies and other components subsequently included in the Spare Parts contract. The parts identified during these purchases provided input for development of the subsequent Spare Parts Contract."

Pg. 16, Par. 1 and Table 5

EPA suggests the following sentence be added as the second sentence to the first paragraph in this section on page 16: "Just prior to release of our draft report to OAR and OAM, EP-D-12-003 was awarded on December 12, 2011 for RadNet Air Monitor Maintenance to Environmental Dimensions, Inc. This contract replaced EP-D-08-068 and does include disincentives for subpar performance as follows: A five (5) percent reduction on the invoiced labor amount for every one (1) percent slippage from the ninety-five (95) percent performance level." EPA also requests that Table 5 be updated to show this disincentive as a Yes.

Pg. 17 (Planned Disincentives Not Included in Spare Parts Contract)

EPA offers the following text to provide additional information for this section:

The procuring CO, Rodney-Daryl Jones was interviewed by Marcia Hirt-Reigeluth, OIG/USEPA on May 23, 2011 and the only discounts mentioned were those dealing with volume discounts included on the parts schedule. The Procurement Initiation Notice (PIN) – Spare Parts Acquisition for RadNet Fixed Monitors contained a parts schedule which identified the parts and estimated quantities. A SOW was not provided with the PIN, this being a commodity acquisition. The program office did not provide a SOW or any document containing disincentives.

A new contract will be established prior to the end of FY 2012 for RadNet Fixed Monitor Spare Parts addressing incentives/disincentives, monthly progress reports and current parts forecast incorporating historical monitor failure data, which was previously not available. The current contract EP-D-10-085 was established with a five year estimate of $1,369,482.00.

Pg. 20, Par. 1

In the first paragraph on page 20, EPA requests that the second sentence be changed to include that the contract is now awarded rather than being a future contract. EPA suggests the sentence read: "The September 2011 version of the SOW for the RadNet service contract awarded in December 2011 contains language to address the proprietary issue."

Pg. 20, Next to Last Par.

EPA notes that the new spare parts contract will contain requirements for MPRs.

Pg. 20, Last Par.

EPA notes that the RadNet air monitor maintenance contract, EP-D-08-068 provided more than adequate reporting through the requirements contained in the SOW and detailed invoicing requirements. A monthly report of the repairs would only be a compilation of the previously submitted individual reports and would have added no additional value.

EP-D-08-068 SOW Task 1.6

Within 7 days of completing on-site maintenance and repair of a monitor, the Contractor shall provide a written report to the COR describing; date of on-site service request; date of on-site service performance; name of service technician performing on-site maintenance and repair; specific monitor deficiencies reported to the Contractor; specific monitor deficiencies encountered by the Contractor; steps and procedures performed to return the monitor to fully functional and calibrated condition; itemization and cost of parts required to return the monitor to a fully functional and calibrated condition; itemization of billable hours related to the on-site maintenance and repair.

Pg. 28, Table

The table entry for compensation received for Modification 4 of delivery order 1 is incorrect. Two MABs were received, not LPUs.

Distribution

Office of the Administrator
Assistant Administrator for Air and Radiation
Assistant Administrator for Administration and Resources Management
Acting Director, National Air and Radiation Environmental Laboratory
Director, Office of Acquisition Management, Office of Administration and
      Resources Management
Agency Follow-Up Official (the CFO)
Agency Follow-Up Coordinator
General Counsel
Associate Administrator for Congressional and Intergovernmental Relations
Associate Administrator for External Affairs and Environmental Education
Audit Follow-Up Coordinator, Office of Air and Radiation
Audit Follow-Up Coordinator, Office of Administration and Resources Management

www.ingramcontent.com/pod-product-compliance
Lightning Source LLC
Chambersburg PA
CBHW081755280526
45789CB00008B/2870